THE COLORING BOOK OF
AMERICAN MODERNIST ARTISTS

RICK KINSEL

LINE DRAWINGS
PAULA KINSEL

MERRELL
LONDON · NEW YORK

in association with

COLORING AMERICAN MODERNISM

These American modernist paintings from the Vilcek Collection provide an outstanding, hands-on introduction to some of the greatest American art of the early twentieth century. Our hope is that, through the images in this book, you will experience firsthand the joyful and innovative use of color for which the American modernist movement is best known.

During the first four decades of the twentieth century, a loose-knit group of artists now known as the American modernists began to abandon existing styles of representation and to create a bold new vision for American art. The ideas that inspired these artists had initially developed in Europe—mostly in France and Germany—but this new work was different in that it specifically addressed American interests and concerns.

The United States was at that time undergoing a period of rapid change: everyday life was accelerating thanks to major advances in industrial technology. The American landscape was changing, too: cities were increasing in size and scale, and skyscrapers, factories, and highways were replacing the farms of the previous century. People were living more closely together than ever before, and were also being drawn together by new kinds of mass media. At the same time as they adopted new and experimental forms of visual representation, the American modernists were responding to the tumultuous changes taking place across America. Some attempted to reconnect with nature, while others fully embraced modernity and progress.

This is the first coloring book ever made of American modernist paintings, and we hope that, by responding to these artworks—either by copying the vibrant palettes of the originals, or by finding inspiration in their colors and designs—you will get a better sense of what it means to be creative and visionary. For this reason, we encourage anyone who colors in this book to create their own "modernist" response to these paintings.

Simultaneously, we hope that art-lovers will take some time simply to appreciate the beauty and imaginative nature of these masterworks—for even today, roughly a century after their creation,

they remain astoundingly impressive.
And since many of the paintings in this
book are abstract in style, but even so
contain recognizable imagery (including
landscapes, buildings, people, and still
lifes), they offer would-be artists a great
introduction to new ways of seeing the
world. In the end, that's what is at the heart
of this collection of American modernist
paintings: the individual artist responding
to what they see and feel, and, in doing so,
turning the commonplace into something
exciting and new.

We have arranged the book thematically,
loosely grouping the paintings into four main
categories: landscapes, buildings, still lifes,
and abstractions. This arrangement makes
it possible for you to wander from the work
of one artist to that of another, just as you
might do in a museum, the better to enjoy
the similarities and differences in the paintings. At the end of the book is a
page listing each painting's artist (including their life dates), title, date of creation,
media, and dimensions.

What strikes me most about the American artists included in this book—
George Copeland Ault, Oscar Bluemner, Howard N. Cook, Andrew Dasburg,
Marsden Hartley, Louis Lozowick, Stanton Macdonald-Wright, Jan Matulka,
Morgan Russell, and Max Weber—is that they all came from different cultural
backgrounds. America enabled and supported their creative work, and, in time,
each artist generously gave back to America by redefining American identity
and creativity.

We invite you to enjoy this splendid and diverse painting collection—and to
have fun creating some new modernist masterpieces!

RICK KINSEL
President, The Vilcek Foundation

3

Jan Matulka · *Indian Dancers* · c.1917–18

Marsden Hartley · *Lost Country—Petrified Sand Hills* · 1932

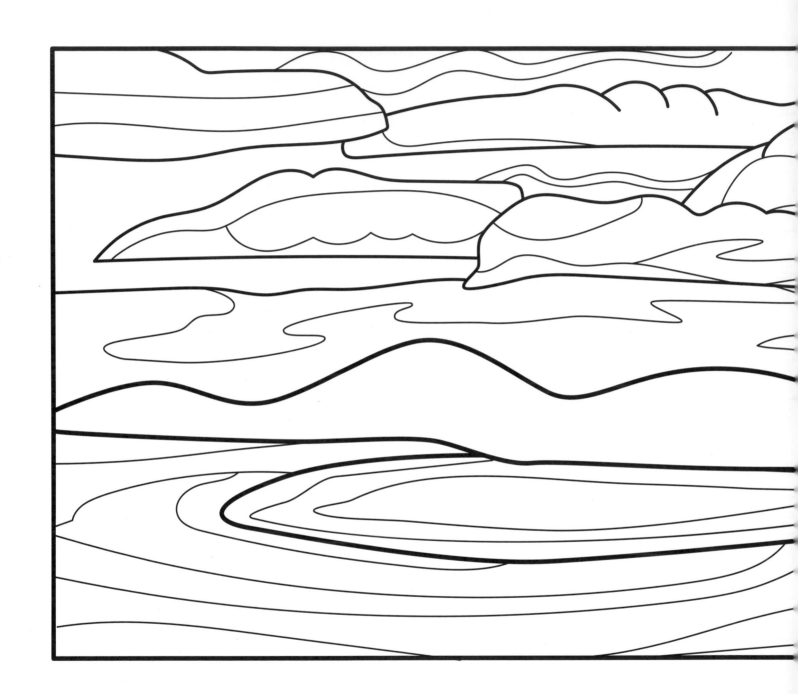

Marsden Hartley · *New Mexico Recollection* · 1923

Marsden Hartley · *Schiff* · 1915

11

Marsden Hartley · *Berlin Series No. 1* · 1913

Andrew Dasburg · *Placita Sanctuario* · 1924

Andrew Dasburg · *Ledoux Street, Taos, New Mexico (Harwood)* · c.1922

Oscar Bluemner · *Red Night, Thoughts* · 1929

Oscar Bluemner · *Young Tree in a Red Courtyard* · 1919

George Copeland Ault · *View from Brooklyn* · 1927

Howard N. Cook
· *Complex City* ·
1956

George Copeland Ault · *New York Night, No. 2* · 1921

George Copeland Ault · *Sunday Afternoon, Greenwich Avenue* · 1925

Andrew Dasburg · *Bryn Mawr* · 1933–35

Louis Lozowick · *Red Circle* · 1924

Oscar Bluemner
· *Perth Amboy West
(Tottenville)* ·
1911, 1916–17

Marsden Hartley · *Atlantic Window in the New England Character* · *c.*1917

Andrew Dasburg · *Portrait of Alfred* · c. 1920

Andrew Dasburg
· *Untitled (Still Life with Artist's Portfolio and Bowl of Fruit)* ·
*c.*1914–18

Max Weber · *Still Life with Bananas* · 1909

Marsden Hartley · *Indian Pottery* · c.1912

Max Weber · *Mexican Statuette* · 1910

Andrew Dasburg · *Modernist Floral* · 1921

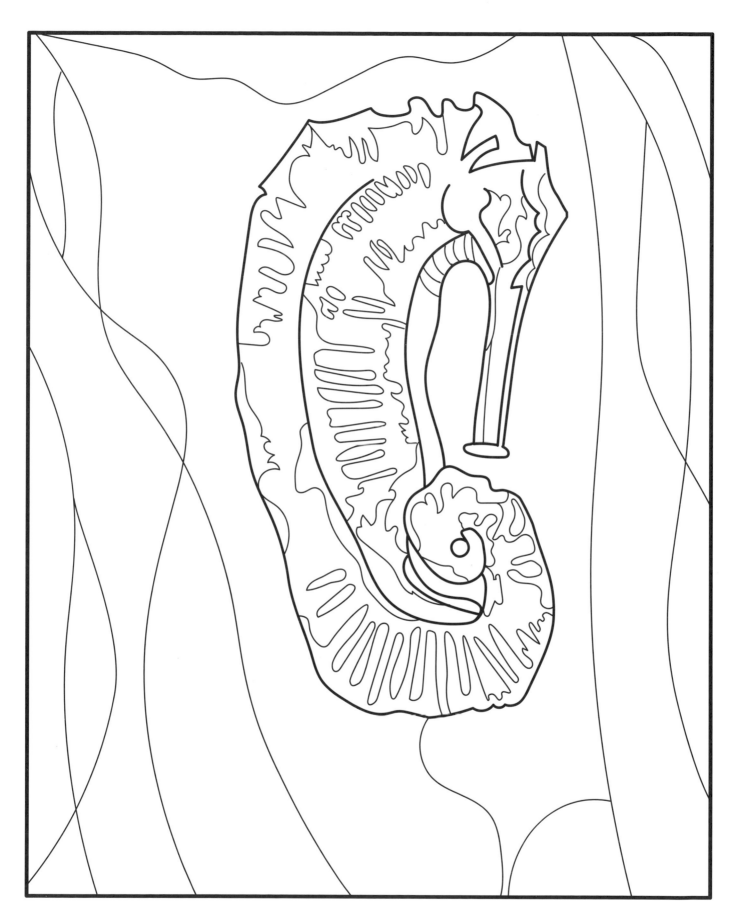

Marsden Hartley · *White Sea Horse* · 1942

Marsden Hartley · *Three Shells* · c.1941–43

Jan Matulka · *Still Life with Owl and Violin* · 1927

Marsden Hartley · *Roses for Seagulls that Lost their Way* · 1935–36

Stanton Macdonald-Wright · *Gestation #3* · 1963

Morgan Russell · *Synchromy* · 1913–14

Marsden Hartley · *Portrait Arrangement No. 2* · 1912–13

LIST OF WORKS

Dimensions indicate height followed by width.

p. 5
Jan Matulka (1890–1972)
Indian Dancers, c. 1917–18
Oil on canvas
26 x 16 in. (66 x 40.6 cm)
Vilcek Collection, 2008.03.01.
Courtesy of the Estate of Jan Matulka

p. 7
Marsden Hartley (1877–1943)
Lost Country—Petrified Sand Hills, 1932
Oil on Masonite
22¼ x 28½ in. (56.5 x 72.4 cm)
Vilcek Collection, 2018.01.01

pp. 8–9
Marsden Hartley (1877–1943)
New Mexico Recollection, 1923
Oil on canvas
12¾ x 32¼ in. (32.4 x 81.9 cm)
Vilcek Collection, 2008.06.01

p. 11
Marsden Hartley (1877–1943)
Schiff, 1915
Oil on canvas with painted frame
39¾ x 31⅞ in. (101 x 81 cm)
Vilcek Collection, 2015.05.01

p. 13
Marsden Hartley (1877–1943)
Berlin Series No. 1, 1913
Oil on canvas board
18 x 15 in. (45.7 x 38.1 cm)
Vilcek Collection, 2012.01.01

p. 15
Andrew Dasburg (1887–1979)
Placita Sanctuario, 1924
Oil on panel
13 x 16 in. (33 x 40.6 cm)
Vilcek Collection, 2008.01.01

p. 17
Andrew Dasburg (1887–1979)
Ledoux Street, Taos, New Mexico (Harwood), c. 1922
Oil on paper board
12⅞ x 16¼ in. (32.7 x 41.3 cm)
Vilcek Collection, VF2016.03.05

p. 19
Oscar Bluemner (1867–1938)
Red Night, Thoughts, 1929
Oil on board mounted on panel
8 x 10 in. (20.3 x 25.4 cm)
Vilcek Collection, 2008.04.01

p. 21
Oscar Bluemner (1867–1938)
Young Tree in a Red Courtyard, 1919
Watercolor on paper
19 x 14 in. (48.3 x 35.6 cm)
Vilcek Collection, 2010.05.02

p. 23
George Copeland Ault (1891–1948)
View from Brooklyn, 1927
Oil on canvas
18¼ x 21½ in. (46.4 x 54.6 cm)
Vilcek Collection, 2007.01.03

pp. 24–25
Howard N. Cook (1901–1980)
Complex City, 1956
Oil on canvas
32 x 44 in. (81.3 x 111.8 cm)
Vilcek Collection, VF2015.05.16

p. 27
George Copeland Ault (1891–1948)
New York Night, No. 2, 1921
Oil on canvas
20¼ x 14 in. (51.4 x 35.6 cm)
Vilcek Collection, 2015.02.01

p. 29
George Copeland Ault (1891–1948)
Sunday Afternoon, Greenwich Avenue, 1925
Oil on canvas
29 x 23 in. (73.7 x 58.4 cm)
Vilcek Collection, 2019.01.01

p. 31
Andrew Dasburg (1887–1979)
Bryn Mawr, 1933–35
Oil on canvas
22¼ x 30⅛ in. (56.5 x 76.5 cm)
Vilcek Collection, VF2020.01.01

p. 33
Louis Lozowick (1892–1973)
Red Circle, 1924
Oil on canvas board
18 x 15 in. (45.7 x 38.1 cm)
Vilcek Collection, 2014.04.01.
© Louis Lozowick; Courtesy of the estate of the artist and Mary Ryan Gallery, New York

pp. 34–35
Oscar Bluemner (1867–1938)
Perth Amboy West (Tottenville), 1911, 1916–17
Oil on canvas
21¼ x 30¼ in. (54 x 76.8 cm)
Vilcek Collection, 2014.02.01

p. 37
Marsden Hartley (1877–1943)
Atlantic Window in the New England Character, c. 1917
Oil on board
31⅝ x 25 in. (80.3 x 63.5 cm)
Vilcek Collection, 2005.04.01

p. 39
Andrew Dasburg (1887–1979)
Portrait of Alfred, c. 1920
Oil on canvas mounted on Masonite panel
22 x 17 in. (55.9 x 43.2 cm)
Vilcek Collection, VF2015.05.18

p. 41
Andrew Dasburg (1887–1979)
Untitled (Still Life with Artist's Portfolio and Bowl of Fruit), c. 1914–18
Oil on canvas
20 x 24 in. (50.8 x 61 cm)
Vilcek Collection, 2004.03.01

p. 43
Max Weber (1881–1961)
Still Life with Bananas, 1909
Oil on canvas
32¼ x 26 in. (81.9 x 66 cm)
Vilcek Collection, VF2018.01.03

p. 45
Marsden Hartley (1877–1943)
Indian Pottery, c. 1912
Oil on canvas
20¼ x 20¼ in. (51.4 x 51.4 cm)
Vilcek Collection, 2006.05.01

p. 47
Max Weber (1881–1961)
Mexican Statuette, 1910
Gouache on paper
29 x 24 in. (73.7 x 61 cm) (sight)
Vilcek Collection, 2005.02.02

p. 49
Andrew Dasburg (1887–1979)
Modernist Floral, 1921
Oil on paper board
16 x 12 in. (40.6 x 30.5 cm)
Vilcek Collection, VF2020.02.01

p. 51
Marsden Hartley (1877–1943)
White Sea Horse, 1942
Oil on Masonite
28 x 22 in. (71.1 x 55.9 cm)
Vilcek Collection, 2013.05.01

p. 53
Marsden Hartley (1877–1943)
Three Shells, c. 1941–43
Oil on board
22 x 28 in. (55.9 x 71.1 cm)
Vilcek Collection, 2012.04.02

p. 55
Jan Matulka (1890–1972)
Still Life with Owl and Violin, 1927
Oil on canvas
40½ x 36 in. (102.9 x 91.4 cm)
Vilcek Collection, VF2017.03.01.
Courtesy of the Estate of Jan Matulka

p. 57
Marsden Hartley (1877–1943)
Roses for Seagulls that Lost their Way, 1935–36
Oil on board
16 x 12 in. (40.6 x 30.5 cm)
Vilcek Collection, 2013.02.01

p. 59
Stanton Macdonald-Wright (1890–1973)
Gestation #3, 1963
Oil on plywood
23½ x 19⅝ in. (59.7 x 49.9 cm)
Vilcek Collection, VF2016.03.14.
Courtesy of the Estate of Jean Macdonald-Wright

p. 61
Morgan Russell (1886–1953)
Synchromy, 1913–14
Oil on canvas
18 x 15 in. (45.7 x 38.1 cm)
Vilcek Collection, VF2019.01.03.
Image courtesy of the Joyce family estate

p. 63
Marsden Hartley (1877–1943)
Portrait Arrangement No. 2, 1912–13
Oil on canvas
39½ x 31¾ in. (100.3 x 80.7 cm)
Vilcek Collection, 2005.09.01

First published 2020 by Merrell Publishers, London and New York

Merrell Publishers Limited
70 Cowcross Street
London EC1M 6EJ
merrellpublishers.com

in association with

Vilcek Foundation
21 East 70th Street
New York, NY 10021
vilcek.org

Text copyright © 2020 Vilcek Foundation
Illustrations copyright © 2020 Vilcek Foundation, with the exception of those noted in captions above, and photograph of colored pencils on cover: © iStock.com/worldofstock
Design and layout copyright © 2020 Merrell Publishers Limited

A catalogue record for this book is available from the Library of Congress.

British Library Cataloguing in Publication Data. A catalogue record for this book is available from the British Library.

ISBN 978-1-8589-4693-1

Produced by Merrell Publishers Limited

Printed and bound in China

Front cover and back cover frame: Marsden Hartley, *Schiff*, 1915; see p. 11.
Back cover, left: George Copeland Ault, *Sunday Afternoon, Greenwich Avenue*, 1925; see p. 29.
Back cover, right: Jan Matulka, *Indian Dancers*, c. 1917–18; see p. 5.
Page 2: Jan Matulka, *Still Life with Owl and Violin* (detail), 1927; see p. 55.
Page 3: Howard N. Cook, *Complex City* (detail), 1956; see pp. 24–25.

RICK KINSEL is President of the Vilcek Foundation.
PAULA KINSEL is an artist, graphic designer, and art director.